THE ADVENTURES
OF RAMA

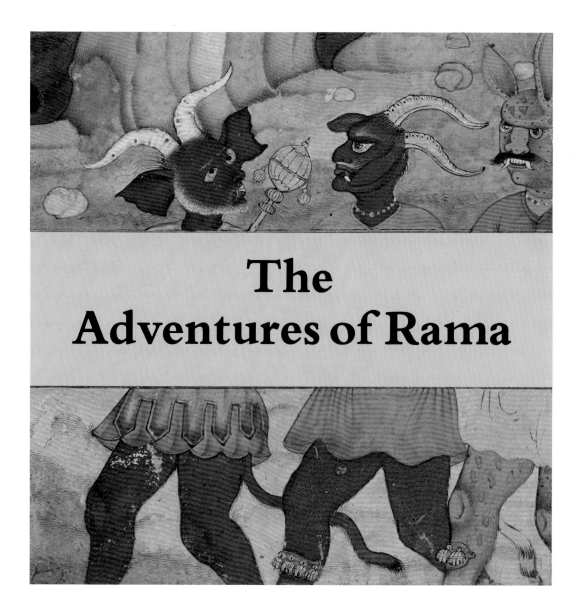

The Adventures of Rama

MILO CLEVELAND BEACH

With Illustrations from a
Sixteenth-Century Mughal Manuscript

Freer Gallery of Art · Smithsonian Institution · Washington, D.C.

*Publication of this book was made possible by a
generous grant from the James Smithson Society of the
National Associates of the Smithsonian Institution.*

FIRST PRINTING, AUGUST 1983
SECOND PRINTING, JANUARY 1985

Library of Congress Cataloging in Publication Data
Beach, Milo Cleveland.
The adventures of Rama.
Adapted from the Rāmāyana.
1. Illumination of books and manuscripts, Mogul—
Juvenile literature. 2. Rama (Hindu deity)—Art—
Juvenile literature. 3. Vālmīki. Rāmāyana—Illustrations—
Juvenile literature. I. Râmâyana (Old Javanese kakawin)
II. Freer Gallery of Art. III. Title.
ND3247.B37 1983   745.6'7'0954   83-1473
ISBN 0-934686-51-3

PRINTED IN THE UNITED STATES OF AMERICA

For Olga, Toby and Sophie, and for Thatcher

THE ADVENTURES
OF RAMA

THE MAJOR CHARACTERS

Dasaratha	*King of Ayodhya; the father of Rama.*
Hanuman	*The general of the army of monkeys.*
Jambhavan	*King of the bears.*
Kaikeyi	*One of Dasaratha's wives; Rama's stepmother.*
Kumbhakarna	*A gigantic demon; brother of Ravana.*
Lakshman	*A brother of Rama; his closest friend.*
Rama	*A son of Dasaratha; an incarnation of the god Vishnu.*
Ravana	*A ten-headed, twenty-armed demon; brother of Kumbhakarna.*
Rishyashringa	*A young holy man.*
Sita	*A daughter of the king of Videha; wife of Rama.*
Sugriva	*King of the monkeys.*
Taraka	*A demoness.*
Vishnu	*The Hindu god of preservation, who is born on earth as the heroic Rama.*
Vishvamitra	*An aged holy man.*

THE MAJOR PLACES

Ayodhya	*The kingdom ruled by Dasaratha; Rama's home.*
Lanka	*The island home of Ravana; also known as Ceylon or Sri Lanka.*
Videha	*The home of Sita.*

WITHOUT DOUBT, Ayodhya was the most beautiful city in all of India. Its wide streets were shaded by stately trees, houses were tall and spacious, and cool streams meandered through groves of mango and of the brilliant tree called Flame of the Forest. Peacocks roamed wild, while friendly monkeys raced through overhead branches. It was an ideal, peaceful world, ruled by a wise and just king.

Despite all this, there was unhappiness and worry. King Dasaratha was growing old, and none of his wives—he had several—had presented him with a son, someone to inherit and protect the kingdom in years to come. After much discussion and thought, he decided to conduct a special ceremony, a sacrifice to the gods, during which he would ask for an heir. His counselors began to search for a holy man to conduct the rites and almost immediately returned with stories of a young hermit named Rishyashringa.

He was a young man who lived deep in the forest, they said, in a hut of branches and leaves that he himself had built. He knew no human beings except for his father; wild animals were his only friends. He had never felt greed or jealousy and spent his time thinking of the gods and wondering how the heavens could be better than life on earth. The gods had long ago decided that Rishyashringa was a saint and rewarded him with special powers: wherever he traveled, a gentle rain would fall invisibly, making plants greener and flowers more abundant.

Dasaratha, intrigued, asked his counselors to inquire further. They learned that Rishyashringa had recently come to the nearby kingdom of Anga. The monsoon rains had bypassed Anga and it had been suffering from drought. Its king had also heard about the saint and had realized that Rishyashringa could restore life to his dry and dying lands. Since the gods would have been angry if the youth had been taken from his home by force, the king of Anga had decided to play a trick. He had chosen the most beautiful women in the land and had sent them to the forest hermitage dressed in sparkling jewels and thin silks. Rishyashringa had been enchanted. He had never seen a woman before, and he willingly followed when they led him to Anga.

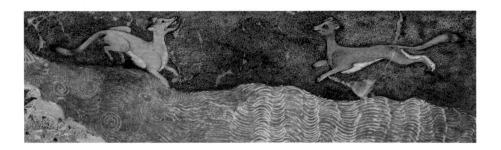

When he heard this story, King Dasaratha decided immediately to ask Rishyashringa to perform the ceremony he had planned, for he was certain that the gods would then look especially favorably upon his request for a son. He went to Anga, where the saint had remained, and when the two returned to Ayodhya, the kingdom was already preparing for the festivities. An occasion of such importance would last many days, and thousands of visitors—even from distant lands—would come. Special houses had to be built for kings and princes, while enormous decorated tents of silk and cotton were set up in the parks; even stables had to be constructed, for the guests would arrive riding elephants, camels, and horses. Servants prepared cooked foods, cool drinks, and mounds of fresh fruit, while musicians and dancers came, hoping for an invitation to perform. Luxury and comfort were provided for everyone, since this was also an occasion to praise and honor the gods.

At long last, the ceremony began. Dasaratha, with his wives and advisers, sat in a special pavilion. Built from fragrant woods and painted by the finest artists, it was filled with soft pillows and hung with flower garlands. Nearby, Rishyashringa and other priests chanted hymns and placed offerings—flowers and grain—in a special sacrificial fire. Transformed into smoke, the offerings rose to the heavens and were received by the gods.

Far above the earth, the three great gods—Brahma the Creator, Vishnu the Preserver and Shiva the Destroyer—sat quietly looking down on Dasaratha's efforts, as they did on every sacrifice. They noticed whether the chants, invocations, or offerings were correctly performed or if the priests were not concentrating. They watched to see if Dasaratha provided lavishly for the comforts and needs of his guests or if he were holding back his wealth and generosity. This ceremony seemed perfect, however. The gods were pleased and paid careful attention—at least until a group of divinities and immortals rushed in noisily and interrupted. They were upset at events happening elsewhere on earth.

The demon Ravana was on the rampage again, they complained, destroying towns and crops, causing storms and droughts, and attacking sages and holy men to upset their prayers. (It was through prayers and offerings from earth that the gods drew their energy.) Ravana was a gigantic monster, with ten heads and twenty arms, and he rode in a magic chariot. His strength and its speed had filled him with pride and arrogance, and none of the lesser divinities singly or even together could defeat him. They therefore begged the great gods for help.

Vishnu immediately decided to be born on earth as a son of Dasaratha, thereby also rewarding the king by granting his wish for an heir. Dasaratha, of course, knew nothing of this.

🌱 🌱 🌱

بابک کوس وموی پروریش اولغایت درازوهمه علامت او دال بربزرکی وکسوت
دبودتادربرافکنده و قدوقامتش مانند قلة که میبریلند وروشنی اوجون شعاع افتاب وچهره
افروختهٔ اوجون طلای که درانش هائنته باشد و فتی که ازانش براٙمده طبعی ازطلای خالص درست

The moment Vishnu had made his decision, a tower of flame burst from Dasaratha's sacrificial fire. For one instant, the entire world seemed as bright as the sun. The crowds rose in terror and pandemonium reigned! The flames whirled and spun, as if around a column, and as they cooled they formed a gigantic manlike creature. He held a bowl, which he handed to the king, and, with a voice louder than nearby thunder, commanded that Dasaratha give the contents to his wives to drink. Then he vanished—totally. The rites were finished.

The queens eagerly drank from the bowl, and soon four sons were born: Rama, Bharata, Lakshman, and Shatrughna. They grew up brave and handsome, beloved by their father and the people of the kingdom. Rama, however, was everyone's favorite, and Lakshman was his constant companion.

One day, when the boys were sixteen, the aged Vishvamitra came to court. He too was a holy man and had traveled from a distant land. As any just and generous king would, Dasaratha welcomed him and promised him whatever he might wish.

Vishvamitra quietly said that he was being tormented by Ravana and was no longer able to perform his prayers. Ravana continually sent demons and ogres to stamp on the fires, blow away the prayer books, and steal the offerings.

The king asked how he could help, and Vishvamitra humbly begged for Rama, saying that he needed a strong and virtuous youth to chase the demons away from his hermitage.

Dasaratha was stunned. He had waited so long for a son that now he did not want to live without Rama at his side; yet he knew that he had to fulfill the sage's request, for he had promised. Since Dasaratha could not dissuade Vishvamitra, Rama—followed as always by Lakshman—left with the frail old ascetic. The king wept.

They traveled along rivers and through forests, sleeping sometimes in hermitages, sometimes just under piles of leaves. For Rama and Lakshman this was an exciting adventure, and from Vishvamitra they learned many things as they walked.

He warned them of the demons they might see, one of whom lived along the path they were following. This was the evil Taraka, and they had no trouble recognizing her forest home: the sky had gradually become gloomy, and the air heavy and dank; then all birds and animals disappeared. Rama, who had never in his life been afraid, became more alert and attentive than ever before.

In the stillness, the only sounds were those of twigs snapping as they moved cautiously forward; yet Taraka heard the travelers. A gigantic spotted monster, she rushed at them, hissing and snarling and hurling rocks. Rama tried to scare her off, but when Vishvamitra begged him to kill her, Rama refused. No matter what, Taraka was a woman and therefore entitled to respect. But

then her attacks became so vicious that Rama had no choice. He quickly and easily shot her with an arrow, and as she died, the forest sprang to life again.

(As a child Taraka had been particularly beautiful and gentle. She married and had a son, Maricha. Her husband soon died, how-

ever, and both Taraka and the child went mad with grief. Unable to control their emotions, they jealously attacked the sages and ascetics who had learned such control. When they threatened Agastya, the greatest of holy men, he condemned Taraka to wear forever a shape that matched her tormented mood. She became a fiend, with hanging breasts and fiery eyes, while Maricha was transformed into an ugly giant. Together they raged through the woods causing senseless destruction.)

24

The gods and forest animals applauded Rama's deed, for it proved his strength and bravery. Celestial weapons and armor were sent to the youths, that they might have divine protection for future battles.

The journey continued, and as the days passed, the heat grew more and more intense. Heavy blossoms hung limply from the trees, and streams dried up from the lack of rain.

Vishvamitra was exhausted when they finally arrived at his home, but he decided anyway to begin his prayers immediately. Although it was now the very hottest part of the summer — which in India is very hot indeed! — he built a ring of fire and sat in the center, proof for the gods that he could endure any hardship in his devotion to them.

The ceremony was long and complicated. For five days and nights he chanted, counting his prayers on a rosary of beads and never once speaking to Rama or Lakshman. He even tied a cord around his knees so he would not collapse from exhaustion. The boys, sitting nearby, were awake and watching the entire time, but there were no interruptions. As the sixth and last day approached, they both wondered whether the demons would actually appear.

At daybreak, it remained almost as black as night, and Rama knew the time of danger had come. Dark shapes moved ominously across the sky, while the wind roared and groaned. Then it began to rain—a downpour not of water but of blood! Lakshman was terrified, but Rama watched fascinated, showing no surprise when two immense demons suddenly appeared. It was Maricha, Taraka's son, with his companion Suvahu. They were bloated and covered with spots, and their tongues hung out of their mouths like snakes stuck in their teeth. They snatched at Rama's weapons and Vishvamitra's offerings, but Rama, quicker than time, aimed his bow and shot the monsters dead.

Vishvamitra had been so absorbed that he never noticed the storm or the demons, and he was astonished when Rama showed him their lifeless bodies. Once again the gods were delighted, for by this act Rama had confirmed his divinity. Vishvamitra, too, praised Rama.

🌱 🌱 🌱

The ceremony completed, the holy man and the youths traveled to Videha, for its king was celebrating an important sacrifice. Vishvamitra also wanted Rama to see an ancient bow, so strong and heavy that no human could shoot arrows from it. It had been given to the king of Videha by the gods in reward for bravery, and the king had promised his daughter Sita in marriage to any man

آن راه عرضدانشت بی شور در دریا افتاد با محمد در مجبند چون او را دید که بهوش نیست

who could shoot the weapon. But it was a trick, for he hoped to keep Sita always nearby.

After a single glance at the princess, Rama effortlessly lifted and shot the bow. He and Sita had fallen in love instantly, and her beauty and gentleness perfectly matched his strength and bravery. Even Sita's father could see that Rama would be a perfect husband, so the two were married amid joyous celebrations.

Dasaratha traveled to Videha for the ceremonies and then returned with the couple to Ayodhya. Delighted by the marriage and by Rama's safe return, he announced that he wished to retire; Rama could then be king, and he, Dasaratha, could devote himself to prayer and the gods.

Throughout the kingdom there was further rejoicing—with one exception. Within her palace quarters, Kaikeyi brooded. She was the mother of Rama's half brother Bharata, and she thought it an insult that her son would not rule. And, alas, she had a weapon to help her ambition: as a reward, Dasaratha had once promised her two wishes, but she had never yet used the gift. She now went to the king and demanded that Rama be exiled to the forests and that Bharata be made ruler.

Dasaratha almost fainted with rage. Once again he knew that he would have to obey or else face the wrath of the gods. But he cursed Kaikeyi.

Rama was banished from Ayodhya for fourteen years, and no one was more upset than Bharata, for he loved Rama and had no

wish to be king himself. All of Ayodhya watched sadly as a royal chariot drove the prince, together with Sita and Lakshman, to the borders of the kingdom. But Rama had always been at home in the forest. He understood the reasons for his exile, and he felt no resentment.

Barefooted and with no belongings other than the clothes on their backs, the travelers wandered through the forests, for they had been forbidden to visit towns or cities. One day, along a narrow pathway, they met a hag—an extraordinarily ugly woman dressed in filthy rags, her hair caked with slime and her breath like old garbage. She begged Rama and then Lakshman to marry her, but they just laughed—and she became so furious that she fled to her brother, who happened, unfortunately, to be Ravana the demon. She told him of the insult and jealously described the beauty of Sita and her devotion to Rama. Ravana vowed revenge. He had heard of Rama and was delighted to have a new person to attack.

In the forest, Rama and Lakshman found a clearing and built a small house. There one day, as Sita was gathering wild fruits and plants for the evening meal, she noticed a beautiful golden deer. She begged Rama to catch it, and he followed it deep into the forest. Noticing that its hooves never really touched the earth, Rama was suddenly certain that it was a demon. He quickly shot the animal, wondering why it had led him off. As it died, it cried for help in a human voice that sounded exactly as if Rama himself were wounded. Lakshman heard it and ran in search of his brother.

While both men were gone, the twenty-armed Ravana came, seized Sita, and carried her off.

noyed them, and they began to give chase, but Hanuman, laughing, easily escaped. He moved farther and farther into the heart of the city, and finally, in a small and almost completely hidden garden, he saw the abducted Sita. She looked pale and thin and sat weeping under a tree. Around her were demonesses of unbelievable ugliness, and they were guarding her carefully. While Ravana had stolen and hidden her, he had also ordered that she not be injured in any way. He hoped, in fact, that Sita would eventually fall in love with him and had tried to persuade her that Rama had given up the search and forgotten her.

So excited by his discovery that his teeth were chattering, Hanuman jumped into the tree. Aware of the rustling of leaves, Sita looked up, and Hanuman saw that she was still as beautiful as a goddess. The monkey softly whispered that Rama was on his way.

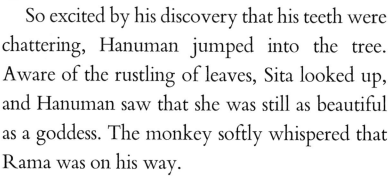

درختان اسوک بن ویران کردن قلعه را ۱۰۹

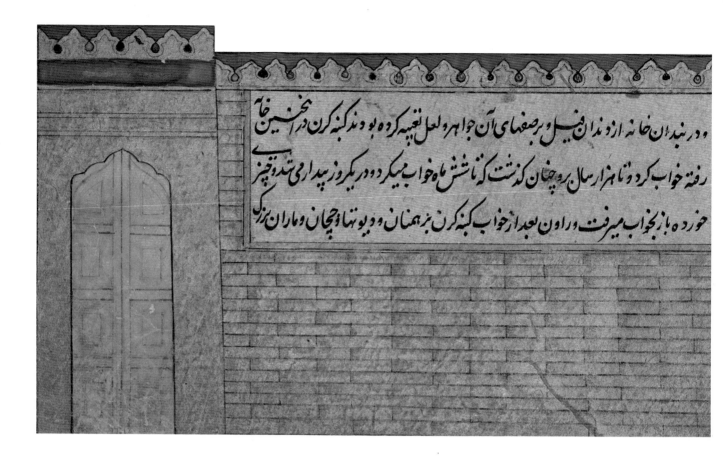

Hanuman quickly returned and told Rama of his adventures. Before they could decide on a plan of attack, the animals, instantly piling up stones and making a bridge, crossed the sea and laid siege to Lanka. Fighting Ravana's troops was no easy task, however, for the island was covered with demons, all armed with magic weapons. Nonetheless, Rama's armies were powerful, and they caused so much damage so quickly that Ravana, watching from the palace, decided to awaken his gigantic younger brother Kumbhakarna and send him into battle.

Kumbhakarna was truly huge. Even lying down, he seemed to touch the sky, and his snores filled the universe. Moreover, he needed almost all the food on earth to fill his vast stomach, and for that reason he had been condemned to sleep six months for every day that he was awake.

Not surprisingly, rousing Kumbhakarna was an ordeal. Mountains of fresh meat were piled near his head so that the smell might awaken him—but there was no response. Hundreds of demons blew trumpets and beat drums. They put ladders against him and climbed onto his stomach, hitting him with clubs and kicking him. He barely noticed. Elephants stood on his chest and sprayed him with water from their trunks, and finally sensing something unusual, Kumbhakarna rose up hungrily. Learning of Rama and his armies and of their threat to his brother, he angrily rode out to battle.

The contest was furious. Monkeys swarmed over him, biting him and trying to pull him down—a hopeless task. Kumbhakarna

attacked them viciously, seizing and devouring the animals by the handful—which meant by the thousands—yet this did nothing to stop his hunger and his rage. Hanuman threw giant boulders, but he might as well have been attacking a mountain. Kumbhakarna seized Sugriva and dragged the monkey king, wounded and unconscious, around the entire battlefield. He was sure the monkey armies would flee if Sugriva, their king, were killed, so he wanted all the monkeys to see what was happening.

بر مینمایند و کینه کردن همه زیور ها بسته و رسول بدست کرد فرشته شوق چالاکی در داشت مانند نا

نمودن گرفت و راون را در بغل گرفت و او را بدست راست وداد کرد و دید و برپای او

و از انجا روان شد و راجی از برای او رابه آورد که مانند راه دیو تا بمقدار پشت دست

در ازی می آن بود و هزار خرابرا حمی کشید ند و برق جنگ براین بسته بودند و مانند ابر صد مکر

و مانند کوه کلاس می نمود و هشت پایه داشت و بسیار نیز رو بود و راجی بخهین ابه برا همره ورد

Sugriva, however, awoke and magically grew as big as the monster. He bit Kumbhakarna's ears and crunched the bones of his nose, and in his pain Kumbhakarna attacked everyone in sight—demons and giants as well as monkeys and bears. To save themselves the monkeys climbed onto Kumbhakarna's back so that he couldn't see them.

The demons then decided to kill Rama; maybe then, all the armies would leave. Rama saw the giant coming towards him and stopped tending the wounds of his friends. Calmly he took an arrow—one of the celestial weapons—and shot it at the beast. Kumbhakarna crashed to earth. While the armies rejoiced, Ravana, mourning the death of his brother, screamed that the attacks were to increase.

The demons responded: they became so ferocious that Rama's troops began to despair. Kumbhakarna's death had been no help, and the demon magic provided continuous trouble and surprises. One example was Ravana's son: he was able to make himself invisible and to travel almost as fast as light, so his attacks sometimes seemed to come from different directions at the same time. He wore Rama's armies out. Exhausted and wounded, they collapsed, thinking that the battle was over.

Hanuman alone, however, was still full of life and energy, and he refused to admit defeat. Rushing from one group of warriors to another, he tried to lift everyone's spirits. It did little good, so the monkey made a quick decision. With lightning speed, and smiling, he jumped over the ocean and all of India and arrived at the Himalaya Mountains in the far north. He had once heard of a magic mountain hidden among the rocky peaks. It was said to be covered with healing herbs, plants that could cure any wound, and Hanuman vowed to find it and bring herbs to Rama and his friends.

Surrounded by wild animals and snakes, he searched. When it grew dark, he stood on a towering crag and gazed over the vast range. One isolated peak was visible in the distance. It was covered with plants, and they glowed with a light of their own. There, Hanuman rejoiced, was his goal.

An impetuous and impatient monkey, Hanuman realized that it would take time to pick all the herbs he needed. Instead, he broke off the entire mountain on which they grew, held it high, and jumped back to Lanka with it.

When he saw Ravana's golden citadel and the battleground covered with dying animals, Hanuman paused in midair. There was no space big enough to set the mountain down. As he hesitated, the smell of the herbs wafted to the warriors, revived them, and cured their wounds. As if nothing had happened, they were ready to charge again into battle, so Hanuman quickly returned the mountain to its home.

Rama, however, was concerned because the animals' faithfulness to him had produced only misery and pain for them. He spoke with the bears and monkeys and begged them to return to their homes to save themselves. He was sure he could manage somehow.

The animals refused. Even if Rama was having doubts, they were not. They knew what was right to do: defeat the demons and rescue Sita—only then would the earth and the gods be safe. And Rama, relieved and delighted, knew that this decision would give everyone new energy.

The battle began again. Hanuman uprooted trees and used them like cudgels, and he broke off mountain peaks and threw given him by the God of Death, but Lakshman's were victorious, and Indrajit, too, was killed. Within the palace, Ravana wept.

With both his brother and his son slain by Rama's forces, Ravana knew that it was time for him to enter the battle. The two armies watched as he descended from the palace tower, where he had been directing the troops. They knew that this was the climactic moment, for the defeat or victory of Ravana himself—and not just of his demonic hordes—would alone be decisive!

Rama and Ravana faced each other, each with more weapons than could be counted. They shot flaming arrows and threw battle-axes. They beat each other with maces and hurled spears and daggers. As Ravana became more and more enraged, Rama grew calmer, further infuriating the demon. His twenty arms moved so fast and so wildly that he looked like a whirlwind, and his ten mouths grunted and roared.

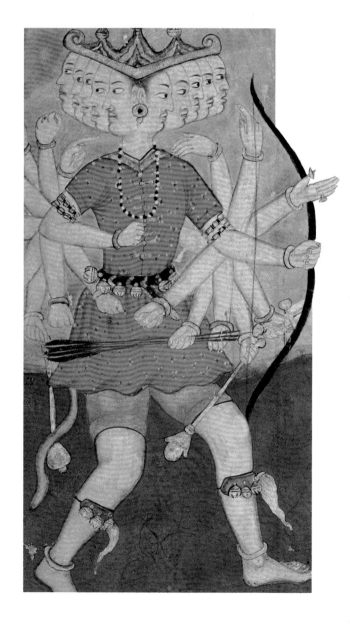

Lakshman, meanwhile, attacked Ravana's chariot and wounded the driver. Ravana, whose heads saw in every direction at once, shot a spear that pierced Lakshman through the heart, and Lakshman fell. For Rama the world turned black, and the battle again seemed to be lost; if his brother died, even victory would bring no joy. He realized how astonished he had been at Lakshman's heroism. His brother had always been gentle, never wanting to hurt a living creature. Rama knew that Lakshman had been showing him his love and devotion.

With great care, Rama slowly removed the spear and asked the gods to spare his brother. They did. Lakshman revived, and the battle went on. But Rama decided that now he himself had to confront and kill Ravana.

He found the spear that had been given him by the god Brahma: a strong, sharp shaft that could travel faster then lightning. Aiming carefully, he shot it at Ravana, and the ten-headed

وجن از جان از قالب راون برآمد و بر زمین چنان افتاد که بر تیر اسپ را زخم انداخته بود و کمان

و تیر از دست او برآمد و در زمین افتاد و وقتی که احسان صاحب خود را کشته و افتاده دید به هر طرف

آرخیند دهیموان خوشحال شده آواز ها کرده بزد و از هر طرف این غلغله برآمد که راون کشته شد رام

demon collapsed, weapons still in every hand. Some of the monkeys came to take revenge on his body: others, whooping joyously, chased the evil armies as they fled terrified from the field. Their leader had died!

🌱 🌱 🌱

After Lakshman, Hanuman had become Rama's greatest friend, and he seemed always to know the right things to say and do. As soon as Ravana uttered his last groans, the monkey raced through the palace to the hidden garden and told Sita of the victory. At once she was transformed. Happiness brought color and life to her face, for Rama had rescued her and proven his love. Hanuman wanted to slay the demon ogresses, but Sita refused to allow more slaughter. After all, she pointed out, they were simply obeying orders and she hadn't been harmed.

After bathing and adorning herself with silks and jewels, Sita went to meet Rama. Together with Lakshman and Hanuman, they climbed into Ravana's magic chariot and flew back to Ayodhya. The fourteen years of exile were over, and Rama, the incarnation of Vishnu, would soon become king. For the time being, gods and men were safe.

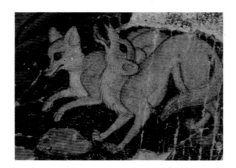

NOTES ON THE TEXT AND ILLUSTRATIONS

The *Ramayana*, one of the great epics of Hindu India, was first written down in Sanskrit about 500 B.C., but even then it was an ancient tale—it had been transmitted orally for centuries by village storytellers. Popular throughout India, the story was told in different regions of the subcontinent in different ways, emphasizing parts that were of special interest to local villagers or incorporating local traditions. Thus, there is no one correct text, although the most popular version is now certainly that of Tulsi Das, who wrote in Hindi and died early in the seventeenth century.

The present work, although drastically shortened, is derived from a sixteenth-century translation of the text into Persian, a project ordered by the Mughal emperor Akbar the Great. In some cases, Persian text panels are visible in the illustrations reproduced. Akbar was only thirteen when his father died and he inherited the throne of a newly established kingdom centered at Delhi, in north India. He was a foreigner and his religion was Islam, although most of the country he ruled was Hindu. Eager to learn the customs and beliefs of his subjects, he had translations made of major Hindu myths, epics, and religious texts, among which was the *Ramayana*. Once a copy was written out by his scribes and illustrated by his painters, Akbar ordered the nobles of his kingdom to make additional copies to place in their own libraries, so that familiarity with such stories would spread throughout Mughal territories.

The paintings reproduced here are all taken from a late-sixteenth-century manuscript now in the Freer Gallery of Art (accession number 07.271). The volume, a copy of Akbar's translation made for the commander in chief of the imperial armies, Abd-ar-Rahim, *Khan Khanan*, contains one hundred thirty paintings. Only twenty-three are included in this book. The list below gives their titles, folio numbers, and painters' names (when known). Unless specifically noted, details rather than full-page views of the original paintings have been used. Also, since these illustrations have been chosen for visual effectiveness, minor episodes of the story sometimes take precedence over major events. This is itself, however, an accepted and traditional approach to *Ramayana* narrations.

54	"View of a Town" from *Rama Removing Ravana's Spear from Lakshman* (fol. 265r).
55	*Rama Removing Ravana's Spear from Lakshman* (fol. 265r).
56	*The Death of Ravana* by Fazl (fol. 270r).
57	"Foxes" from *Rama and Lakshman Fight the Demoness Taraka* by Mushfiq (fol. 35r).

Two excellent and more extensive, but still abridged, retellings of the *Ramayana* in English are generally available and highly recommended:

> R.K. Narayan, *The Ramayana*. New York, 1972.
> William Buck, *Ramayana*. Berkeley and Los Angeles, 1976.

A full translation of the lengthy Sanskrit version by the poet Valmiki has also been published:

> Hari Prasad Shastri, trans. *The Ramayana of Valmiki*.
> London, 1962.

For a scholarly discussion of the Freer manuscript, see:

> Milo Cleveland Beach, *The Imperial Image: Paintings for the Mughal Court*. Washington, D.C., 1981, pp. 128–55.

And, finally, an excellent and lively introduction to Mughal India can be found in:

> Bamber Gascoigne, *The Great Moghuls*. London, 1971.

ACKNOWLEDGMENTS   The author wishes especially to thank Dr. Thomas Lawton, Director, Freer Gallery of Art, for his enthusiastic endorsement of this project; and Richard Louie, Assistant Director, for editorial advice and support. Klaus Gemming, the designer, was a constant source of information and ideas, and the effectiveness of the layout is tribute to his skills. Elizabeth Gemming provided excellent and thorough copy editing.

THE ADVENTURES OF RAMA

was designed by Klaus Gemming, New Haven, Connecticut.
The text was set in Monotype Bembo, a typeface designed
about 1495 for the Venetian printer-publisher Aldus Manutius
by the engraver and goldsmith Francesco Griffo. The typeface
was named for Cardinal Pietro Bembo, an Italian humanist.
The composition is by A. Colish, Mount Vernon, New York.
The book was printed in four-color process lithography
by Princeton Polychrome Press, Princeton, New Jersey, on
Lustro Offset Enamel Dull coated paper, made by the
S.D. Warren Company, a division of the Scott Paper Company,
and bound by A. Horowitz & Sons, Bookbinders, Fairfield, New Jersey.

FREER GALLERY OF ART